School Puzzles

HIGHLIGHTS PRESS
Honesdale, Pennsylvania

Welcome, Hidden Pictures® Puzzlers!

When you finish a puzzle, check it off ✓. Good luck, and happy puzzling!

Contents

School Spirit

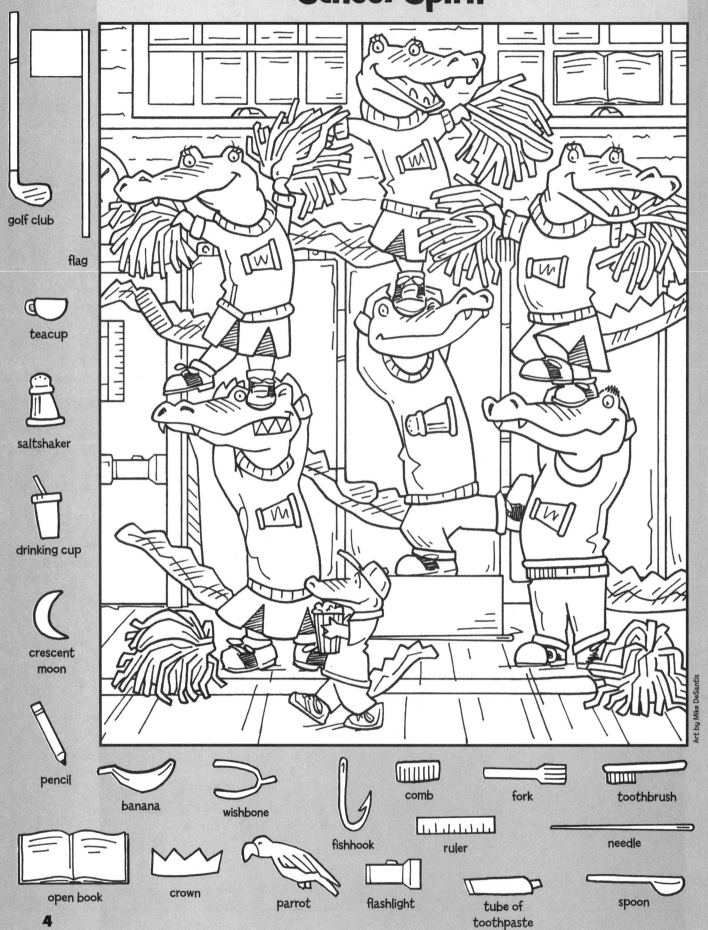

golf club

flag

teacup

saltshaker

drinking cup

crescent moon

pencil

banana

wishbone

fishhook

comb

fork

toothbrush

ruler

needle

open book

crown

parrot

flashlight

tube of toothpaste

spoon

Art by Mike DeSantis

4

Cafeteria Chaos

Art by Diana Zourelias

tent

baseball bat

bell

cup

lollipop

candy cane

scissors

worm

crescent moon

Paint

nail

needle

screw

leaf

teacup

duck

stick

mushroom

fish

clothespin

flashlight

boomerang

Teacher Appreciation Day

snake

ax

brush

banana

fishhook

boomerang

doughnut

canoe

clamshell

E
the letter E

Art by Ellen Appleby

Science Fair Winner

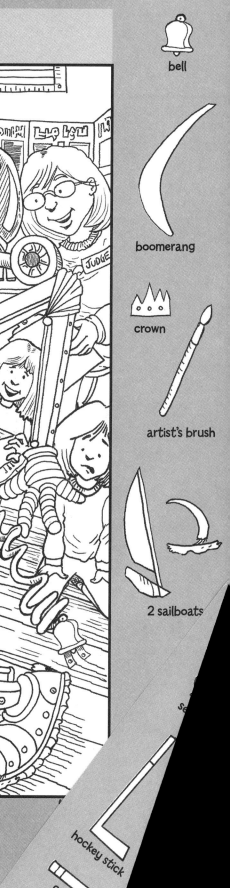

bell

boomerang

crown

artist's brush

2 sailboats

hockey stick

crayon

8

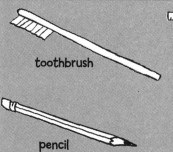

toothbrush

ruler

comb

domino

pencil

fish

slice of bread

cup

Off to School

mallet

spatula

drinking straw

pennant

drinking glass

pointy hat

seashell

Art by Gary Mohrman

fish

magic lamp

whale

dog bone

bell

arrow

slice of pie

yam

heart

goose

Solar Systems

drinking glass

paw print

traffic cone

lollipop

candy cane

musical note

sock

snowman

toothbrush

frying pan

feather

bowl

crown

snake

key

slice of pizza

banana

clock

dragonfly

bell

9

Art by Jennifer Harney

VENUS

MERCURY

EARTH

MOON

Science Experiment

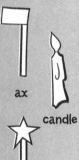

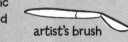

ghost

canoe

ruler

needle

hockey stick

ax

candle

cookie

magic wand

artist's brush

boomerang

carrot

fish

leaf

teacup

banana

magnet

crescent moon

crown

bell

olive

sock

envelope

doughnut

snake

Art by Bill Golliher

Horse Play

crescent moon

baseball bat

carrot

fork

leaf

exclamation point

banana

envelope

snail

snake

fried egg

ghost

cupcake

ruler

Art by Mernie Gallagher-Cole

11

Computer Lab

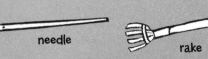
needle · rake

mushroom

scissors

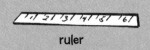
ruler

heart

button

flashlight

paper clip

drinking straw

lock

pencil

shovel

piece of popcorn

artist's brush

leaf

ballpoint pen

doughnut

crescent moon

spatula

postage stamp

adhesive bandage

starfish

broom

screwdriver

ice-cream bar

lollipop

nail

slice of watermelon

fishhook

bell

envelope

comb

teacup

caterpillar

domino

School Cafeteria

ring

glove

ice-cream
cone

paper clip

hourglass

banana

crown

Art by Tim Davis

book

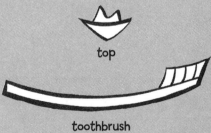

top

toothbrush

sailboat

shoe

Pen Pals

flag

golf club

ladder

candle

crescent moon

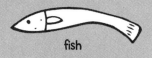
fish

bell

teacup

magnet

pennant

toothbrush

ring

shoe

horn

purse

Art by Mary Sullivan

15

Nestling Flight School

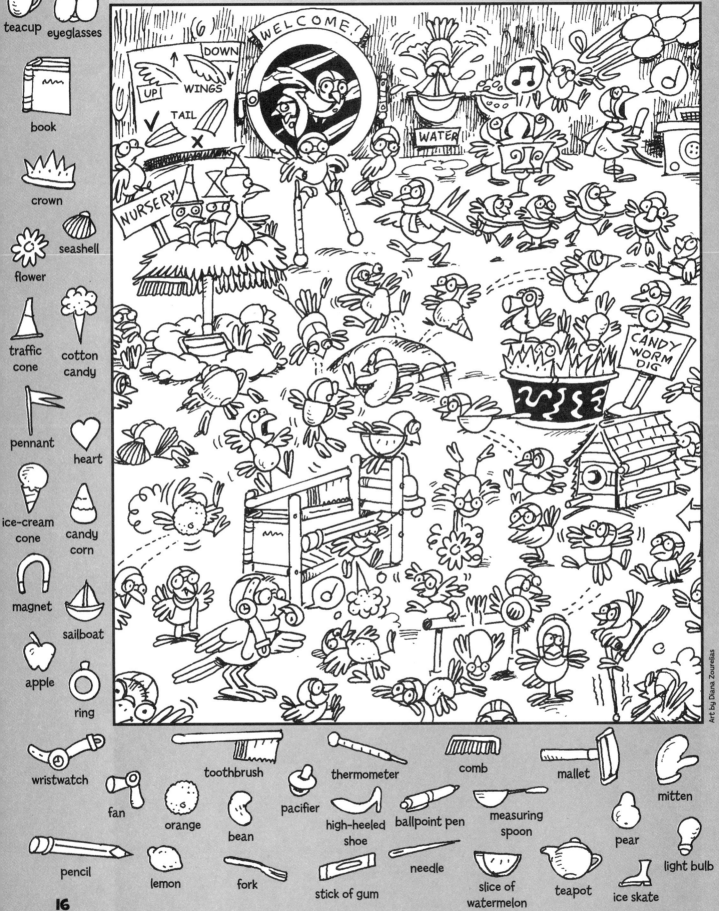

teacup · eyeglasses · book · crown · seashell · flower · traffic cone · cotton candy · pennant · heart · ice-cream cone · candy corn · magnet · sailboat · apple · ring

wristwatch · fan · orange · bean · pacifier · toothbrush · high-heeled shoe · ballpoint pen · thermometer · measuring spoon · comb · mallet · mitten · pencil · lemon · fork · stick of gum · needle · slice of watermelon · teapot · pear · light bulb · ice skate

16

Art by Diana Zourelias

Busy Library

Read Learn Grow

candle

hockey stick

top hat

flag

comb

pennant

crescent moon

lightning bolt

spool of thread

jar

heart

slice of cake

butter knife

pencil

shoe

domino

squash

artist's brush

ruler

wishbone

noodle

pickax

magnet

piece of candy

flashlight

seashell

Art by Gary Mohrman

17

Dog Drawing

flag

hockey stick

slice of cake

shovel

sock

closed umbrella

briefcase

needle

banana

magnifying glass

kite

arrow

ribbon

pear

thimble

snake

ice-cream bar

Art by Sally Springer

18

Advancing to Goal

Art by Neil Numberman

banana

artist's brush

sailboat

ice-cream cone

lollipop

cotton swab

needle

pitcher

ring

book

rabbit

heart

leaf

broccoli

slice of pizza

19

Fish School

balloon

horseshoe

football

funnel

2 + 3 =
4 + 2 =
5 + 1 =

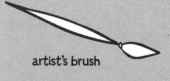
artist's brush

seashell

paper clip

comb

20

snowman

lightning bolt

carrot

crescent moon

bowl

envelope

Art Show

feather

spool of thread

pea pod

broccoli

chili pepper

lemon

boomerang

ring

iron

seashell

thimble

tube of toothpaste

horseshoe

teacup

slice of pie

candy corn

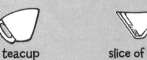
harmonica

ladybug

Art by Susan Dahlman

22

Biggest Brain

ladder

golf club

hockey stick

needle

drinking
straw

fishhook

domino

crown

slice of pizza

heart

shoe

wedge of
orange

comb

crescent
moon

teacup

Field Trip

pennant

spoon

envelope

ruler

canoe

snake

ULTRASAURUS

book

measuring
cup

light bulb

pencil

butterfly

bat

Art by Ellen Appleby

25

Rabbits at Recess

sailboat

2 mushrooms

plate

bell

ruler

snake

kite

banana

slice of pizza

seashell

feather

sock

candle

glove

Art by Tamara Petrosino

Princess and the Frog

candle

banana

book

mushroom

ice-cream cone

Art by Gary Mohrman

slice of pie

heart

egg

boomerang

slice of bread

top hat

spoon

shoe

mitten

needle

28

Shhhhh!

spool of thread

hoe

needle

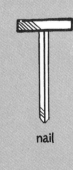
nail

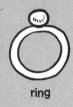
ring

mug

sock

party hat

mitten

boot

comb

sailboat

paper clip

boomerang

Busy Bus

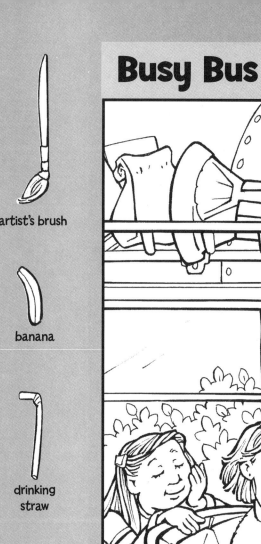

artist's brush

banana

drinking
straw

sock

scissors

dust pan

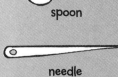
spoon

needle

chef's hat

butterfly

flashlight

slice of
watermelon

heart

kite

ice-cream cone

pencil

bell

nail

lollipop

lock

Art by Ellen Appleby

envelope

fishhook

adhesive bandage

caterpillar

knitted hat

Monkey Bars

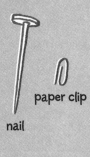
nail

paper clip

flag

candle

mitten

book

banana

shoe

pencil

crown

bell

slice of pie

toothbrush

sailboat

heart

saw

bird

Art by Tim Davis

32

Late for School

boot

ice-cream cone

tape measure

pear

high-heeled shoe

ladder

dinosaur

box of tissues

arrow

slice of pizza

canoe

mushroom

cupcake

tack

Art by Marilee Harrald-Pilz

33

Painting

pennant

needle

butterfly

pencil

sock

sailboat

hockey stick

toothbrush

ruler

telephone receiver

party hat

top hat

domino

ice skate

boot

nail

Art by Karen Stormer-Brooks

School Garden

lollipop

cane

boot

elf's hat

artist's brush

ice-cream cone

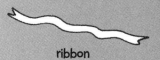
slice of pie

stick of gum

loaf of bread

drinking glass

seashell

ribbon

fish

staple

canoe

Art by Gary Mohrman

35

Art Model

screwdriver

candle

sailboat

spool of thread

ice-cream bar

mushroom

pencil

bow tie

spatula

lock

diamond

slice of pie

slice of pizza

butterfly

drinking glass

book

crescent moon

36

Art by David Helton

Bus Stop

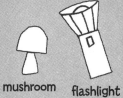
mushroom

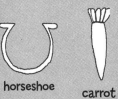
flashlight

horseshoe

carrot

slice of cake

sock

baby's rattle

fan

pear

wedge of orange

spool of thread

leaf

ball of yarn

button

fried egg

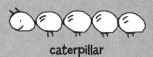
caterpillar

spoon

dog bone

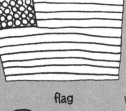
flag

ruler

envelope

fish

wedge of cheese

kite

37

Choir Concert

belt

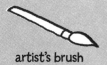
magnifying glass

artist's brush

ear of corn

mushroom

toothbrush

slice of pie

needle

drinking
straw

roller skate

harmonica

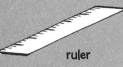

golf club   ruler

Art by Neil Numberman

Paper Pals

banana

heart

eyeglasses

sailboat

crescent moon

comb

egg

saw

mug

toothbrush

stick of gum

roller skate

fish

Art by Tim Davis

40

Cafeteria

ruler

baseball bat

crescent moon

house

pencil

bird

bat

fish

domino

acorn

tube of toothpaste

sailboat

light bulb

worm

handbell

Art by Maggie Swanson

41

Student Art Show

saltshaker

needle

candle

crayon

artist's
brush

pencil

nail

saxophone

comb

crescent
moon

flipper

spoon

ruler

musical note

mug

fishhook

crown

toothbrush

banana

duck

book

Art by Mike DeSantis

42

School Swim Team

pine tree

glove

leaf

heart

balloon

lollipop

baseball

banana

rolling pin

ruler

mustache

megaphone

vase

crescent moon

golf club

toothbrush

ring

spoon

envelope

tube of toothpaste

worm

mitten

peanut

slice of pizza

hockey stick

crown

Art by Gary LaCoste

Soccer Team

drinking straw

kite

golf club

hot dog

cupcake

candy corn

pencil

seashell

paintbrush

ice-cream
bar

mushroom

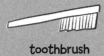
toothbrush

book

mug

Art by Barry Gott

45

Arts and Crafts Day

golf club

celery

pair of shorts

sock

Art by Scot Ritchie

hamburger

loaf of bread

chef's hat

sailboat

cotton candy

heart

doughnut

clamshell

saltshaker

mug

cherries

fried egg

46

Book Sale

golf club

kite

spatula

candle

sailboat

mallet

ruler

slice of pie

sock

envelope

toothbrush

horseshoe

pencil

snake

Opening Act

crescent moon

party hat

banana

heart

bowl

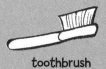
spool of thread

toothbrush

fish

Art by Rocky Fuller

Class Crafts

carrot

cane

bell

envelope

fried egg

feather

candle

boot

hot dog

ladder

screwdriver

loaf of bread

handbag

pear

dog bone

belt

tennis racket

arrow

toothbrush

banana

frying pan

Art by Mernie Gallagher-Cole

49

Science Fair

golf club

drinking straw

lollipop

closed umbrella

bell

iron

crown

flute

hammer

four-leaf clover

nail

leaf

key

glove

paw print

bucket

VINEGAR

BAKING SODA VINEGAR CO2

VOLCANO

50

What
Do
Plants
Need
To
Grow?

ROBOTICS

Art by Laura Ferraro Close

mallet

pencil

musical note

ladder

sailboat

grapes

mushroom

earmuffs

banana

hat

ring

button

megaphone

cupcake

crescent
moon

open book

51

Study Time

needle

cane

artist's brush

pennant

lollipop

funnel

ring

 toothbrush

 telescope

 sock

 heart

 sailboat

 mug

 spoon

 hammer

 crescent moon

 snake

 magnet

 slice of pie

Art by Rocky Fuller

52

Pirate School

needle

ice-cream cone

carrot

canoe

lollipop

spoon

crown

sock

slice of pizza

scissors

book

doughnut

envelope

pear

Art by Paula Becker

53

Heading Home

tomato

pennant

crescent moon

heart

bell

sock

nail

canoe

feather

string bean

envelope

seashell

crayon

butter dish

strawberry

needle

Art by Gary Mohrman

54

Bus Ride

candy cane

shovel

pea pod

drinking straw

screwdriver

oil can

ruler

baseball

magnet

pencil

magic wand

snake

slice of watermelon

skateboard

wristwatch

elf's hat

crescent moon

tube of toothpaste

Art by Ron Zalme

55

Sit, Stay, Learn

matchstick

crescent moon

game piece

boomerang

chili pepper

fish

crown

acorn

baseball bat

drinking
straw

carrot

button

heart

Art by Iryna Bodnaruk

Class Picture

nail

key

hoe

spatula

sailboat

pennant

kite

artist's brush

lollipop

ice-cream bar

slice of pie

sock

slice of pizza

slice of bread

open book

ax

pencil

mallet

mug

cat

needle

ladder

Art by Olivia Cole

Art Show

goblet · ring · ladder · pencil · crayon · arrow · egg · boot · banana · flag · high-heeled shoe · flashlight · artist's brush · ballpoint pen · candle · cracker · box of cereal · book · bean · tent · nail · top · sock · key · ice-cream cone · bowl · heart · tube of toothpaste · drumstick · butter knife · ruler · hat · stick of gum · olive · pretzel · leaf · licorice · light bulb · knitted hat · mushroom · magnet · lemon

Art by Diana Zourelias

Make the Catch

nail

ballpoint pen

candle

golf club

funnel

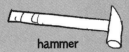

hammer

peanut

envelope

adhesive
bandage

sneaker

bowl

toothbrush

rhino

mitten

dinosaur

rabbit

Art by Chuck Dillon

60

At the Art Museum

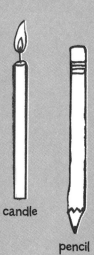
candle

pencil

crescent moon

banana

lollipop

button

spoon

crown

cherry

slice of pizza

candy corn

clock

sock

slice of watermelon

envelope

whale

baseball

fishhook

seashell

Art by Mernie Gallagher-Cole

61

Reading Corner

kite

feather duster

hockey stick

glove

shuttlecock

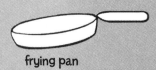
frying pan

slice of pie

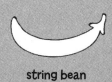
string bean

paintbrush

62

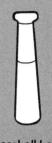
baseball bat

flag

candle

ballpoint pen

pair of pants

elbow noodle

ruler

peanut

leaf

candy corn

Art by Dana Regan

The Librarian

hockey stick

crescent moon

pencil

hat

bottle

shopping cart

key

sailboat

swan

paper clip

leaf

banana

toothbrush

slice of pie

boot

snake

saw

bell

fish

LIBRARY

QUIET PLEASE

CHILDREN'S ROOM

READ IT!

Magic Show

feather

cane

wishbone

mitten

crescent
moon

fan

seashell

ruler

baseball

fried egg

snowman

toothbrush

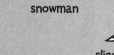
hat

pie

stick of gum

slice of pizza

Prehistoric Playground

needle

nail

necktie

golf club

candle

artist's brush

pennant

ladle

pencil

spoon

banana

wishbone

heart

musical note

fish

carrot

glove

comb

toothbrush

Art by Mike DeSantis

66

Cheerleader Tryouts

LUNCH

TRYOUTS TODAY! 1 PM ~ 3 PM

Art by Diana Zourelias

clothespin

flag

magnet

ice-cream cone

tack

heart

crescent moon

ring

mushroom

candle

egg

saltshaker

button

traffic cone

coin

goggles

bell

olive

ice-cream scoop

teacup

toothbrush

domino

lamp

adhesive bandage

pencil

piece of popcorn

open book

slice of pizza

measuring spoon

flashlight

butter knife

wishbone

slice of watermelon

crown

comb

golf tee

The Zebra High Newspaper

needle

ruler

banana

hammer

pencil

slice of pizza

waffle

wedge of
orange

snake

carrot

candle

ice-cream
bar

ice-cream
cone

saucepan

teacup

comb

heart

plate

Art by Tamara Petrosino

Flight Class

artist's brush

pencil

tack

bow tie

slice of cake

binoculars

button

TODAY'S LESSON: TAKEOFF TIPS

spoon

worm

mug

magnifying glass

bell

fish

carrot

butterfly

glove

East Galaxy School

coin

flashlight

envelope

drinking glass

wedge of orange

slice of watermelon

ring

fried egg

doughnut

slice of pie

bowl

sock

light bulb

horseshoe

banana

Art by Paula Becker

71

Dog Training

golf club

fried egg

hockey stick

pennant

candle

kite

sock

banana

slice of pie

leaf

book

mushroom

bow tie

cupcake

boot

tack

bowl

sailboat

feather

FOOD

NOT FOOD

Lunch 11:30

Art by David Helton

Show and Tell

ice pop

candle

arrow

fish

paper airplane

feather

heart

toothbrush

slice of bread

crown

bowl

mitten

wishbone

canoe

ruler

apple

cupcake

doughnut

bell

Art by David Bernardy

banana

candle

ice-cream
cone

wedge of
cheese

Night School

glove

hat

boomerang

kite

feather duster

heart

slice of watermelon

mustache

cinnamon bun

fish

slice of pie

Art by Tamara Petrosino

75

Marching Band

measuring cup

shoe

pennant

wedge of cheese

seahorse

flag

heart

crescent moon

arrow

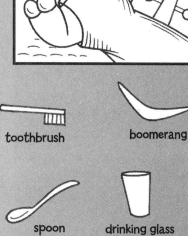

toothbrush

boomerang

sock

pencil

fishhook

tack

spoon

drinking glass

celery

slice of bread

  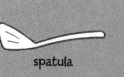
spatula

glove

Art by Gary Mohrman

76

Reading Rabbits

butter knife

bean

mitten

flower

hat

ice pop

adhesive bandage

domino

cracker

comb

toothbrush

butterfly

2 slices of pizza

spool of thread

olive

flashlight

golf tee

pennant

needle

bell

candy cane

crescent moon

slice of bread

heart

lightbulb

pear

mug

lollipop

baseball bat

hot dog

candle

tack

banana

Art by Diana Zourelias

Story Time

bowling pin

banana

bell

snow cone

paper clip

WELCOME
TO
AUTHOR &
ILLUSTRATOR
DAY!

HOUSE

Art by Tim Davis

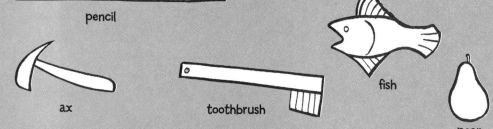

pencil

ax

toothbrush

fish

pear

slice of pie

star

Perfect Pose

baseball bat

boot

sailboat

candle

cotton
candy

kite

hammer

tent

cinnamon
bun

bell

envelope

snail

apple

flute

hat

fish

leaf

knitted hat

teacup

79

Curtain Call

balloon

banana

crown

hockey stick

toothbrush

feather

spoon

ring

fork

snake

saltshaker

comb

key

fish

artist's brush

horseshoe

slice of pie

bowl

pencil

Art by David Helton

Sea School

ladle

doughnut

golf club

boot

hockey stick

sock

ruler

comb

lightning bolt

olive

pennant

funnel

boomerang

paper airplane

canoe

needle

crown

mitten

flashlight

mug

closed umbrella

82

Art by Bill Golliher

Reading Room

baseball bat

closed umbrella

pencil

flashlight

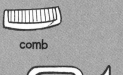
comb

baseball

leaf

wrench

toothbrush

horn

nail

apple

needle

Art by Rocky Fuller

83

Valentine's Day Party

candle

book

cupcake

sock

tack

golf club

key

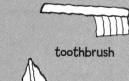
toothbrush

paintbrush

teacup

caterpillar

sailboat

doughnut

worm

84

Going Home

crescent moon

nail

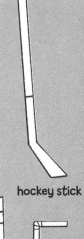
hockey stick

pencil

drinking straw

chili pepper

spool of thread

ruler

lightning bolt

candy corn

slice of pie

thimble

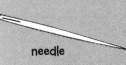
needle

megaphone

broccoli

clamshell

ring

85

Almost Summer

glove

horn

ice-cream cone

hockey stick

paper clip

musical note

heart

T-shirt

toothbrush

hammer

banana

fish

seal

86

Gym Class

closed
umbrella

nail

mug

crescent moon

doughnut

saltshaker

teapot

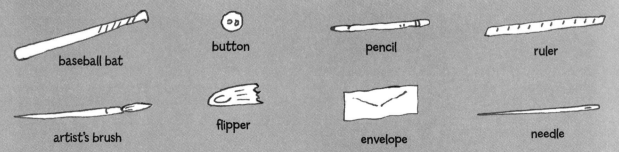

baseball bat

button

pencil

ruler

artist's brush

flipper

envelope

needle

Art by Scot Ritchie

87

Museum Visit

mushroom

banana

balloon

dragonfly

sailboat

ring

pennant

lamp

ice-cream bar

ice-cream cone

shoe

comb

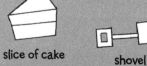
crown

needle

slice of pie

wrench

mallet

screwdriver

crescent moon

slice of cake

shovel

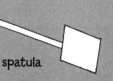
spatula

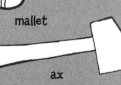
ax

88

Art by Olivia Cole

Bear Band

open book

carrot

pencil

heart

arrowhead

spool of thread

clothespin

ring

butterfly

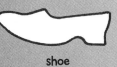
fish

snake

slice of pie

mug

shoe

Art by Maggie Swanson

89

National Craft Month

ladder

shuttlecock

octopus

bird

mouse

butterfly

duck

closed umbrella

cracker

slice of pizza

lightning bolt

star

flashlight

whale

eyeglasses

domino

open book

Fire Safety

pointy hat

fishhook

show cone

measuring cup

mitten

flowerpot

sailboat

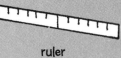
ruler

sock

spatula

mushroom

bell

banana

ladder

flashlight

tube of toothpaste

Art by Elizabeth Allyn Hendricks

drinking straw

golf club

ladle

baseball bat

flashlight

spatula

toothbrush

banana

bell

carrot

needle

nail

tack

teacup

comb

Art by R. Michael Palan

Disk Toss

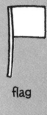
flag

artist's brush

needle

pointy hat

chef's hat

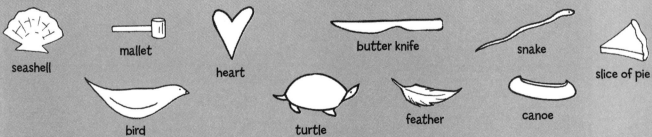

seashell

mallet

heart

butter knife

snake

slice of pie

bird

turtle

feather

canoe

Art by Gary Mohrman

93

Wheels on the Bus

hockey stick

crescent moon

sock

slice of pizza

fish

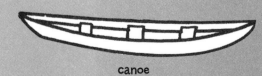
canoe

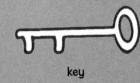
key

tube of toothpaste

94

drinking straw

light bulb

bird

ring

yo-yo

paintbrush

seashell

flashlight

Art by Daryll Collins

95

Class Photo

handbell

ice-cream cone

golf club

candle

boomerang

crescent moon

mug

tulip

duck

bird

fish

butterfly

pencil

ax

96

Dinosaur Museum

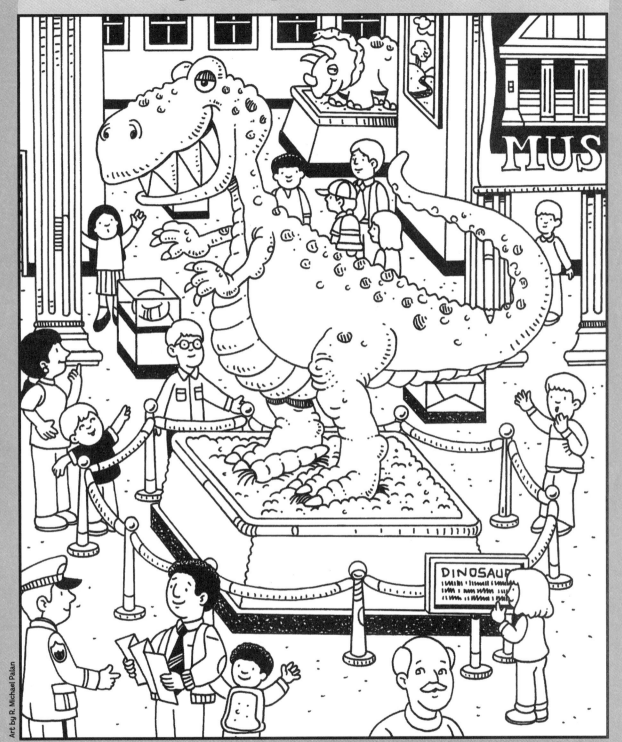

drinking straw

baseball bat

pencil

needle

bell

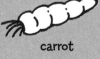
carrot

sock

slice of bread

boot

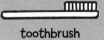
toothbrush

envelope

flashlight

worm

97

Craft Activity

sock

tube of toothpaste

broom

snow cone

heart

flag

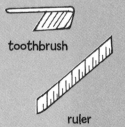
toothbrush

ruler

ring

bottle of lotion

eyeglasses

flashlight

iron

harmonica

crown

98

Touchdown!

banana

fishhook

nail

paper clip

drinking straw

artist's brush

mitten

bat

paddle

thimble

acorn

crown

candle

sneaker

peanut

megaphone

teacup

crayon

Art by Neil Numberman

99

School Crossing

artist's brush

golf club

wristwatch

domino

crescent moon

ring

tube of toothpaste

mug

crown

envelope

pliers

bowl

toothbrush

cotton candy

Art by Ron Lieser

100

The Robot

cherry

carrot

banana

pineapple

slice of
watermelon

grapes

lima bean

peanut

ear of corn

apple

mushroom

pear

Recess

hockey stick

ruler

flag

closed umbrella

handbell

spool of thread

envelope

saw

slice of bread

cupcake

pencil

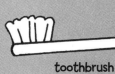
toothbrush

dog bone

tube of toothpaste

baseball glove

mushroom

102

Art by Maggie Swanson

Robo-Dino

OUTDOOR
SCIENCE FAIR
TODAY →

scrub brush

harmonica

wrench

eraser

mug

coin

spoon

crescent
moon

ruler

crown

flag

lollipop

pencil

book

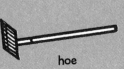
artist's brush

hoe

slice of pizza

carton of milk

tube of
toothpaste

slice of bread

Art by Joe Seidita

103

Crossword Competition

comb

crescent moon

nutcracker

drinking straw

golf club

toothbrush

wrench

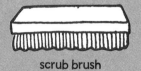
scrub brush

cupcake

magnet

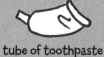
crown

tube of toothpaste

caterpillar

saltshaker

Art by Ron Lieser

Art Homework

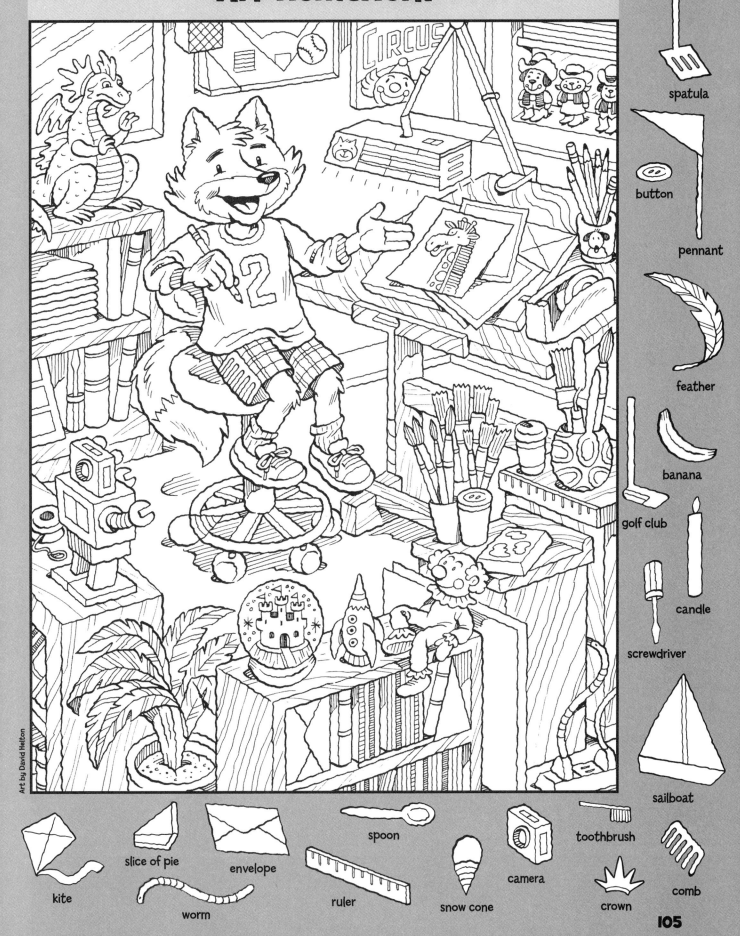

spatula

button

pennant

feather

banana

golf club

candle

screwdriver

sailboat

kite

slice of pie

envelope

worm

spoon

ruler

snow cone

camera

toothbrush

crown

comb

Art by David Helton

105

clothespin

comb

cherry

key

slice of pie

Science Projects

sock

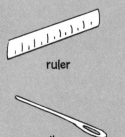
ruler

football

pliers

spoon

needle

paper clip

celery

ring

106

Art by Joseph Wigfield

A Trip to the Zoo

 pencil

zipper

adhesive bandage

screw

artist's brush

diamond

heart

shovel

 worm

apple

 spoon

snail

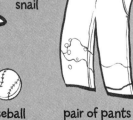 pair of pants

 mitten

cookie

slice of pizza

sailboat

comb

 baseball

 duck

 snow cone

Art by Jennifer Harney

107

Serve's Up!

carrot

baseball bat

sailboat

cherry

eyeglasses

tack

acorn

hockey stick

light bulb

lollipop

slice of pizza

ax

bell

comb

mug

Art by Jackie Stafford

Sweetest Day

Art by Pat Lewis

ladle

baseball bat

drinking straw

crescent moon

kite

carrot

pennant

feather

shoe

sailboat

comb

boomerang

slice of pizza

snail

sock

bird

crown

snake

Higher Learning

pea pod

crescent moon

candle

heart

screw

bell

seashell

fork

wishbone

peanut

artist's brush

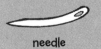
ring

bowl

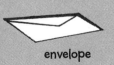
envelope

harmonica

needle

slice of pie

Art by Susan Dahlman

Rainy-Day Dance

hockey stick

candle

trowel

envelope

fishhook

fried egg

acorn

toothbrush

paper clip

yo-yo

snake

slice of pizza

bowl

ruler

wedge of lemon

oil can

bell

Art by Lyn Martin

Science Rules!

wristwatch

banana

rake

artist's brush

ring

slice of pizza

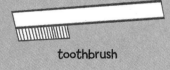
toothbrush

adhesive bandage

mitten

envelope

sailboat

belt

tack

bottle of glue

button

Art by Susan Miller

Attention, Class

Ms. Mitzy

Math

42 + 12 =
34 - 23 =
16 + 64 =
7 x 7 =

12 + 47 + 56 =
90 - 56 - 7 =
120 + 4 ÷ 5 =
200 x 4 x 3 =

Art by René Mitchell-Mills

button

pennant

balloon

cane

candle

lollipop

strawberry

bowl

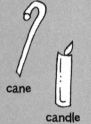
mushroom

tube of toothpaste

oar

heart

scrub brush

toothbrush

needle

whistle

seashell

domino

slice of cake

measuring cup

flower

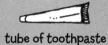

Lady Liberty

ice-cream bar

mushroom

ice-cream cone

teacup

glove

heart

beet

ruler

pencil

acorn

snake

ax

toothbrush

saucepan

envelope

mitten

comb

Art by Neil Numberman

Dodge Ball

hockey stick

fishhook

sock

cotton candy

pencil

candy cane

toothbrush

fork

slice of pie

teacup

horseshoe

ring

boomerang

fish

crown

heart

bell

116

Art by Mitch Mortimer

Butterfly Hike

flower

wishbone

scissors

ring

lock

seashell

ice-cream cone

lemon

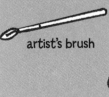
artist's brush

scrub brush

pencil

mitten

canoe

computer mouse

spoon

mug

crown

Art by Ron Lieser

117

Fish Magic

gingerbread
man

elbow noodle

crescent moon

chef's hat

funnel

ice-cream
cone

spatula

glove

Art by Laura Ferraro Close

broccoli

piece of popcorn

tooth

ghost

sock

bell

key

Planetarium Visit

hockey stick

lollipop

horn

yo-yo

heart

banana

flag

tack

teacup

shuttlecock

book

snow cone

wishbone

butterfly

stick of gum

rolling pin

spool of thread

potato

bell

crayon

magnet

slice of pizza

pencil

doughnut

flowerpot

saucepan

sailboat

bean

bowl

Art by Diana Zourelias

Swish!

mitten

banana

drinking straw

kite

feather

toothbrush

slice of pie

pencil

heart

cupcake

envelope

canoe

fried egg

sock

Dinosaur Facts

banana

baseball bat

drinking straw

kite

wrench

ice-cream cone

candy cane

snowman

leaf

egg

pencil

key

snake

puzzle piece

ruler

toothbrush

slice of pizza

heart

ice-cream bar

flag

comb

Art by Jennifer Harney

122

Early Morning

hockey stick

sock

button

lemon

slice of bread

carrot

pear

heart

crayon

SCHOOL BUS

BUS STOP

Art by Josh Cleland

toothbrush

banana

ladle

fish

heart

crayon

ruler

magnifying glass

doughnut

butcher knife

candle

Bookworms

pickax

hat

handbell

heart

sailboat

horn

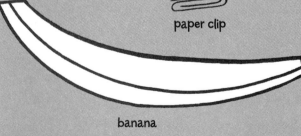
banana

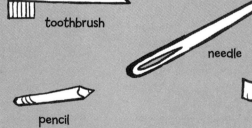
paper clip

toothbrush

needle

pencil

ruler

hockey stick

124

Library Card

drinking straw

golf club

pennant

comb

crescent moon

banana

caterpillar

sailboat

leaf

slice of watermelon

doughnut

bat

toothbrush

envelope

flashlight

crayon

slice of bread

Art by Ellen Appleby

Ready for the Day

tack

crescent moon

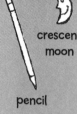
pencil

sailboat

heart

banana

rake

candle

knitted hat

boot

feather

waffle

teacup

slice of pie

light bulb

handbell

comb

canoe

toothbrush

wedge of cheese

ax

fish

caterpillar

bike helmet

snake

Art by Rich Powell

Automatic Cat Feeder

pennant

flag

crescent moon

broccoli

artist's brush

candle

needle

sock

lollipop

comb

nail

sailboat

spoon

envelope

tack

golf club

slice of pie

spatula

mallet

crown

mushroom

Art by Chuck Galey

Hopscotch

balloon

sailboat

lightning bolt

candle

bell

ice-cream bar

mug

crescent moon

sock

envelope

slice of pizza

wedge of lemon

comb

kite

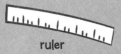

ruler

Art by Tamara Petrosino

128

Taking Notes

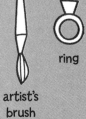
ring

artist's brush

nail

candle

cherry

button

golf club

banana

bell

sock

acorn

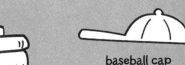
baseball cap

toothbrush

mug

tube of toothpaste

comb

saltshaker

crescent moon

crown

Art by Mike DeSantis

129

Answers

▼Page 4

▼Page 5

▼Page 6

▼Page 7

▼Page 8

▼Page 9

▼Page 10

▼Page 11

Answers

▼ Pages 12–13

▼ Page 14

▼ Page 15

▼ Page 16

▼ Page 17

▼ Page 18

▼ Page 19

Answers

▼Pages 20-21

▼Page 22

▼Page 23

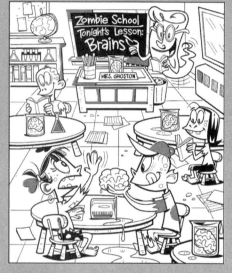

▼Pages 24-25

▼Pages 26-27

▼Page 28

Answers

▼ Page 29

▼ Pages 30–31

▼ Page 32

▼ Page 33

▼ Page 34

▼ Page 35

▼ Page 36

▼ Page 37

Answers

▼Pages 38-39

▼Page 40

▼Page 41

▼Page 42

▼Page 43

▼Pages 44-45

▼Page 46

▼Page 47

▼Page 48

▼Page 49

▼Pages 50-51

▼Page 52

▼Page 53

▼Page 54

▼Page 55

Answers

▼Pages 56-57

▼Page 58

▼Page 59

▼Page 60

▼Page 61

▼Pages 62-63

▼Page 64

▼ Page 65

▼ Page 66

▼ Page 67

▼ Pages 68-69

▼ Page 70

▼ Page 71

▼ Page 72

▼ Page 73

Answers

▼ Pages 74-75

▼ Page 76

▼ Page 77

▼ Page 78

▼ Page 79

▼ Pages 80-81

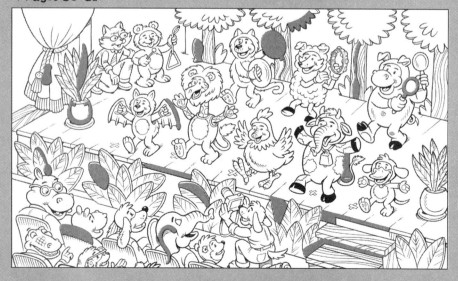

▼ Page 82

▼ Page 83

▼ Page 84

▼ Page 85

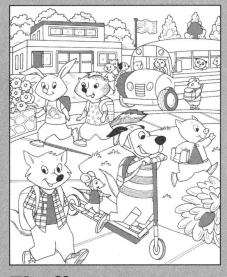

▼ Page 86

▼ Page 87

▼ Page 88

▼ Page 89

▼ Page 90

▼ Page 91

Answers

▼Page 92

▼Page 93

▼Pages 94–95

▼Page 96

▼Page 97

▼Page 98

▼Page 99

▼ Page 100

▼ Page 101

▼ Page 102

▼ Page 103

▼ Page 104

▼ Page 105

▼ Page 106

▼ Page 107

Answers

▼ Pages 108-109

▼ Page 110

▼ Page 111

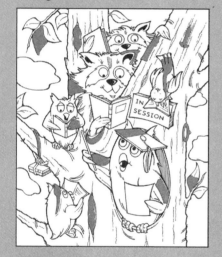

▼ Page 112

▼ Page 113

▼ Page 114

▼ Page 115

▼ Page 116

Answers

▼ Page 117

▼ Page 118

▼ Page 119

▼ Pages 120-121

▼ Page 122

▼ Page 123

▼ Page 124

▼ Page 125

Answers

▼ Page 126

▼ Page 127

▼ Page 128

▼ Page 129

For information about permission to reproduce
selections from this book, please contact
permissions@highlights.com.

Published by Highlights Press
815 Church Street
Honesdale, Pennsylvania 18431
ISBN: 978-1-68437-655-1
Manufactured in Secaucus, NJ, USA
Mfg. 04/2019

First edition
Visit our website at Highlights.com.
10 9 8 7 6 5 4 3 2 1